Witness History Series

THE USSR UNDER STALIN

Stewart Ross

The Bookwright Press
New York · 1991

Titles in this series

The Arab-Israeli Conflict
Blitzkrieg!
China since 1945
The Cold War
The Origins of World War I
The Rise of Fascism
The Russian Revolution
South Africa since 1948
The Third Reich
The United Nations
The United States since 1945
The USSR under Stalin
War in the Trenches

Cover illustration: A Spanish poster from the late 1930s showing Lenin and Stalin.

First published in the
United States in 1991 by
The Bookwright Press
387 Park Avenue South
New York, NY 10016

First published in 1991 by
Wayland (Publishers) Ltd
61 Western Road, Hove
East Sussex BN3 1JD
England

© Copyright 1991 Wayland (Publishers) Ltd

Library of Congress Cataloging-in-Publication Data
Ross, Stewart.
    The USSR under Stalin / Stewart Ross.
        p. cm. – (Witness history)
    Includes bibliographical references and index.
    Summary: Examines the social and economic changes in the Soviet Union during Stalin's regime and discusses the nation's devastation by World War II.
    ISBN 0–531–18409–9
    1. Soviet Union – Politics and government – 1936–1953 –Juvenile literature. 2. Stalin, Joseph, 1879–1953 – Juvenile literature. 3. Heads of state – Soviet Union –Biography – Juvenile literature. [1. Soviet Union – Politics and government – 1936–1953. 2. Stalin, Joseph, 1879–1953.] I. Title. II. Series: Witness history series.
DK268.R67 1991   90–24373
947.084'2–dc20   CIP
                                                            AC

Typeset by Kalligraphic Design Limited, Horley, Surrey
Printed by G. Canale & C.S.p.A. Turin

Contents

BOLSHEVIK RUSSIA

VLADIMIR ILYICH ULYANOV, commonly known as Lenin, suffered the first of several strokes on May 26, 1922. He died less than two years later, age only fifty-three.

Lenin was the inspiration and mastermind behind the Bolshevik revolution of November 1917, which led to the establishment of the Soviet Union as the world's first communist state. The coup in Petrograd (renamed Leningrad in 1924), which had overthrown the short-lived Provisional Government, was followed by a bitter civil war. The Bolshevik Red Army fought against the counter-revolutionary, pro-Czarist White Russians, who were supported by several Western countries, and against provinces

A Bolshevik poster entitled "The First Day of Soviet Rule." Lenin (holding papers) is shown with the revolutionary soldiers, sailors and workers.

The USSR was made up of people of many different races. This government propaganda poster shows a Russian and an Asian woman working harmoniously together.

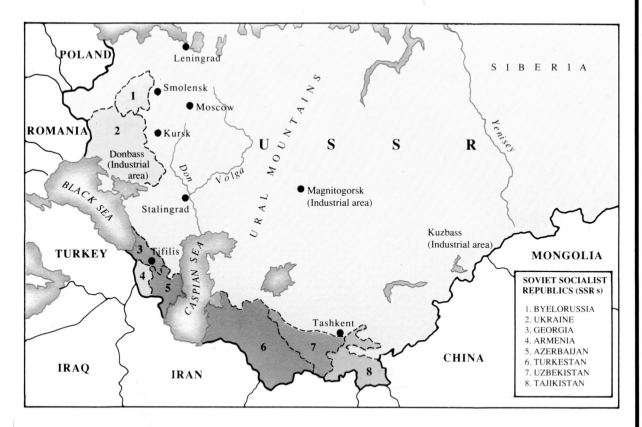

A map of the USSR in 1932, showing the areas that became Soviet Socialist Republics.

of the former empire that sought independence from the Russian government. Some countries, such as Poland and Finland, gained their independence; other areas, such as the Ukraine and Georgia, failed and were absorbed into the Soviet Union. By the end of 1921 the communist state was only slightly smaller than the former empire of the Czars.

As Chairman of the Communist Party, Lenin was largely responsible for the form of the new one-party state. He adapted the ideas of Karl Marx, the German philosopher who had founded modern communism, to suit Russian needs. In 1921 Lenin introduced a New Economic Policy (NEP) to revive the Russian economy, which had been devastated by World War I, the revolution and the civil war. He drew up a democratic constitution for the USSR, but through the secret police (known originally as CHEKA) he ensured that all opposition to the Communist Party was ruthlessly eliminated. In many ways, therefore, the Soviet Union was Lenin's own creation, and his early death left a gaping void at the heart of the system.

Of all the leading members of the Politburo (the controlling organ of the Communist Party), there was one whom Lenin did not wish to succeed him. In 1922–3 Lenin wrote:

> . . . having become General Secretary, [he] has concentrated enormous power in his hands, and I am not sure that he always knows how to use that power with sufficient caution . . . [he] is too rude, and this fault . . . becomes insupportable in the office of General Secretary.[1]

The colleague of whom Lenin was speaking was Joseph Vissarionovich Dzhugashvili. History remembers him simply as Stalin.

1
THE RISE OF STALIN
The man from Georgia

JOSEPH DZHUGASHVILI was born in 1879, the only surviving child of an impoverished washerwoman and her cobbler husband living in Gori, southern Georgia. The boy's life was extremely hard. His home was a two-roomed hovel, he caught smallpox at the age of six (which left him severely scarred), and it is said that he was cruelly beaten by his drunken father.

Naturally ambitious and aggressive, at an early age the young Stalin learned to blot out wounding human emotion. At the funeral of his first wife in 1907 he confessed, pointing to her coffin: "She was the only creature who softened my heart of stone. She is dead, and with her have died my last warm feelings for humanity."[2] Of all the pseudonyms adopted by Joseph Dzhugashvili, the one that stuck was "Stalin;" it means "man of steel."

Stalin was a promising but difficult student; he was expelled from the Theological Seminary at Tifilis in 1899. He joined the Social Democratic Party, a revolutionary Marxist organization, and endured a number of jail sentences and periods of exile in remote parts of the Russian empire. When the Social Democrats split between the Mensheviks and the Bolshevik faction led by Lenin, he sided with the latter. Stalin became a member of the Bolshevik Party Central Committee in 1912.

Stalin was one of the first prominent Bolshevik leaders to enter Petrograd for the Bolshevik uprising of 1917. Lenin noticed the loyal Bolshevik's Georgian background and ability, and appointed him First Commissar for the Nationalities after the revolution. While in this post Stalin acquired influence in the non-Russian areas of the Soviet Union and filled regional posts with people loyal to himself. He served on the southern front during the civil war, and in 1922 he was made General Secretary of the Communist Party. He used the position to accrue considerable power.

It was by no means certain upon Lenin's death that Stalin would succeed him as head of state. Trotsky, Zinoviev, Kamenev and Bukharin all held more senior posts. There were several factors that assisted Stalin in his bid for power:

This picture of the young Stalin in the winter uniform of the Red Army clearly shows his Georgian facial characteristics. Stalin was one of the few early Bolshevik leaders who came from outside Russia.

Molotov, Stalin and Lenin working on *Pravda* (*Truth*). Stalin encouraged the distribution of pictures showing himself with Lenin.

- As General Secretary, he was able to use the Communist Party apparatus to further his ambitions.
- He had proven administrative ability.
- He was an astute politician.
- He came from a genuinely working-class background.
- As a Georgian, who had not learned

Russian until he went to school, he understood the problems of the "nationalities," the non-Russians who made up 50 percent of the USSR's population.

The new leader

Stalin seized power in a very subtle manner. He made few radical pronouncements, and headed no particular group or faction. Instead, he deliberately fostered the image of a moderate, reasonable man who wished only to serve the USSR by following in Lenin's footsteps. In a sense, Stalin hid behind the Party apparatus while he was steadily rebuilding it in his own interests.

Despite Lenin's expressed wish for an ordinary burial, Stalin arranged for his body to be embalmed and put on public display in a special mausoleum in Red Square, Moscow. Stalin played a key role at the funeral of the dead leader, hoping that he would be perceived as the heir apparent. On the evening before the funeral Stalin delivered his famous oration, which began:

> *In departing from us, Comrade Lenin enjoined us to hold high and keep pure the great calling of member of the Party. We vow to thee, Comrade Lenin, that we will with honor fulfill this thy commandment.*[3]

A "cult of Leninism" was initiated, of which Stalin became the high priest, despite the fact that Lenin had often expressed his dislike of the "cult of the individual."

Stalin's power-base lay in the Communist Party apparatus. He immediately began a

A huge banner displayed on Lenin Victory Day in 1987, emphasizing the lasting importance of Lenin in the USSR.

A bust of Lenin in Moscow, the city that was made the capital of the USSR.

recruitment drive, which attracted almost half a million new members to the Party by the end of 1924. He now called the Party the "vanguard of the working class" and "the embodiment of unity of will."[4]

Lenin's death left Trotsky as undoubtedly the ablest member of the Politburo. But he was neither an astute politician nor an easy man to get on with. Many Bolsheviks feared that it was Trotsky, not Stalin, who was trying to establish himself as supreme leader. Stalin used this anxiety to arrange for Trotsky to be relieved of positions of power and eventually driven into exile. In October 1924 Trotsky fell out with Zinoviev and Kamenev, the respective heads of the Party in Leningrad and Moscow. After his resignation as

Commissar for Military and Naval Affairs (in 1925) and expulsion from the Politburo (in 1927), he ceased to be a major political influence. Meanwhile, Stalin had allied himself with Bukharin, the editor of *Pravda*, and had isolated Zinoviev and Kamenev at the Fourteenth Party Congress in 1925.

In 1928 Stalin turned the Party machine against Bukharin, Rykov and Tomsky, who opposed his plans for rapid industrialization. All three left the Politburo in January 1929. By December, when Stalin celebrated his fiftieth birthday, it was clear that the USSR had only one leader. Portraits of "the Lenin of today" adorned the streets, and messages of congratulation poured in from all over the country.[5] The Stalinist era had begun.

"Socialism in one country"

The struggle for power that followed Lenin's death was not just a personal conflict between ambitious individuals. It also involved the difficult process of defining Marxism-Leninism, the USSR's guiding philosophy.

The Bolshevik revolution of October 1917 had been led by a small group of dedicated revolutionaries, who believed that the time was ripe for communist revolutions all over the world, not just in Russia. After World War I there were upheavals in several European countries, during which Soviet-style republics were set up in Bavaria (in Germany) and in Hungary. But these were soon crushed. A socialist uprising in Germany was defeated in 1923; therefore, Russia was left isolated as the only communist state.

Trotsky, who considered himself Lenin's natural successor, believed in "permanent revolution." These were its main aspects:

1 Workers' power was the only way forward for backward Russia.

2 Socialism could not be created in Russia alone because the working class was too tiny and the economy was too backward. It could be achieved only if the large working classes took power in the developed Western countries and shared their resources with communist Russia.

3 Capitalism was an international system, and socialism would be too. To succeed, the revolution had to spread abroad.

A poster supporting the Red Worker (communist) candidate in the 1923 elections in Germany. After World War I there was a real possibility that communism might spread to other countries in the way that the Bolsheviks advocated.

Rival newspapers published during the British General Strike of 1926 expressing two quite different opinions. The failure of strikes to lead to revolution in countries such as Britain strengthened Stalin's argument for "socialism in one country."

Stalin was a pragmatist. He was not an intellectual, but he realized the importance of ideas in furthering his ambitions. As one historian has written:

Stalin's attitude to ideas was utilitarian. If they served to make the Soviet Union stronger they were welcome.[6]

Stalin realized that there were unlikely to be socialist revolutions abroad in the near future.

His alternative was to be "socialism in one country."

"We communists are . . . made of special stuff," he declared.[7] The Soviet Union would create socialism alone. This policy met with approval from the Russian people, who were weary of waiting for revolutions abroad. But in order to survive without support from other countries, the USSR needed to create a strong industrial economy. The peasants, who formed the majority of the population, had to be persuaded or forced to abandon their traditional way of life. The way to do this was to introduce state-controlled industrialization.

2
THE FIVE-YEAR PLANS
A backward state

THE ECONOMIC POTENTIAL of the USSR was enormous. European Russia, lying to the west of the Ural Mountains, was bigger than the rest of Europe. To the east lay a territory twice as large again. The USSR's total land mass was double that of the United States. The thinly-spread population of the Soviet Union (147 million) exceeded that of the U.S. by about 27 million. It was more than twice the size of Germany's population and more than three and a half times that of Britain.

The Soviet Union was also rich in natural resources. The Ukraine contained some of Europe's richest farmlands. From the Black Sea to the Urals and beyond, as far as western Siberia, there were vast deposits of coal, iron and other minerals to be exploited. But the following table reveals the poor performance of Soviet industrial output in 1928, compared with that of several smaller nations.[8]

A propaganda poster showing an idealized vision of peasant life. The Bolsheviks had intended that workers should control their own work but the Five-Year Plans were to ensure that labor was firmly controlled by the state.

	USSR	UK	GERMANY	FRANCE
Wheat (thousands of tonnes)	20,000	1,600	4,000	8,000
Coal (millions of tonnes)	31	227	316	52
Steel (millions of tonnes)	4	7	11	9
Motor vehicles (thousands)	0.8	130	90	135
Electricity (millions of KWh)	5.1	20	27	10
(1 tonne = 1.102 tons)				

A number of economic and ideological problems had to be overcome if the USSR were to achieve the state-controlled industrialization required by the doctrine of "socialism in one country."
- The devastation of 1914–22 had set back the USSR's industry many years. Production did not reach pre-war levels until 1928.
- About 80 percent of the population were peasants, farming small plots of land using methods that had changed little for

hundreds of years. Backward-looking and resistant to change, they resented having to part with their produce at cheap prices to feed the city dwellers.
- The communist USSR was politically isolated and could expect little economic assistance, in the form of investment or technical expertise, from the more developed capitalist nations.
- The NEP had denationalized many industrial plants and permitted farmers to

ВРАГИ ПЯТИЛЕТКИ

ПОМЕЩИК СМОТРИТ ЗЛЫМ БАРБОСОМ, КУЛАК СОПИТ БУГРИСТЫМ НОСОМ, ПЬЯНЧУГА С ГОРЯ ПЬЕТ ЗАПОЕМ, ПОП ОГОЛТЕЛЫМ ВОЕТ ВОЕМ,

ШИПИТ ПРОДАЖНЫЙ ЖУРНАЛИСТ, ОСТРИТ КЛЫКИ КАПИТАЛИСТ, МЕНЬШЕВИЧОК ВО-ВСЮ ЯРИТСЯ, ВОЯКА БЕЛЫЙ МАТЕРИТСЯ,—

ПСЫ, НЕ ПОСАЖЕННЫЕ В КЛЕТКУ, ВСЕ, КТО СТОИТ ЗА СТАРИНУ, ЗЛО ПРОКЛИНАЮТ ПЯТИЛЕТКУ И ОБЪЯВЛЯЮТ ЕЙ ВОЙНУ,

ГРОЗЯТ ЕЙ СРЫВОМ, ПОНИМАЯ, ЧТО В НЕЙ—ПОГИБЕЛЬ ИХ ПРЯМАЯ!

ДЕМЬЯН БЕДНЫЙ.

▲ **A Soviet propaganda poster attacking "enemies of the people" who threaten the success of the Five-Year Plans. The "enemies" include a rich landowner, a priest, a Czarist officer, a Menshevik and a *kulak*.**

Agricultural machinery such as this reaping machine was rare in the 1920s. The introduction of machinery meant that less workers were needed in agriculture, so more could go to work in the new industries.

sell food for profit, as under capitalism. This had undermined the principles of socialism.

Stalin could have continued Lenin's NEP policies, but instead he decided to resume full state control of the economy. In 1929 the Party launched the First Five-Year Plan. It was to bring hardship and starvation to the peasant class.

Industrialization

Stalin's announcement in February 1931 proved remarkably prophetic. Ten years after these words were uttered, the Soviet Union was invaded by Nazi Germany. The Soviets were just strong enough to drive back the invaders.

There were three Five-Year Plans before World War II:

1 October 1929 – December 1932.
2 November 1933–March 1937.
3 March 1938–1942 (disrupted by the outbreak of war in 1941).

The Plans, which were drawn up by Gosplan (the state economic planning agency established in 1921), set targets for industry to achieve. For example, in the First Plan, which concentrated on heavy industry, the output of coal, iron, steel, oil and machinery was to triple; electricity production was to be increased sixfold. The Second and Third Plans placed greater emphasis on defense (32.6 percent of the budget by 1940), transportation and – in theory – consumer goods. Proposals were formally placed before

A woman working in a Moscow ball-bearing factory, 1937.

groups of workers for their approval. The secret police dealt with objectors.[10]

The full force of the state and Party machine was mobilized to ensure that the Plans succeeded. Hundreds of thousands of people were forced to migrate from the countryside to the new cities, where they were hastily trained in new skills. The work-force was tightly controlled. By 1939 unruly workers could be imprisoned and those who missed a day's work dismissed instantly. Theft of state property was made punishable by death. Work-books and internal passports enabled the authorities to direct labor to where it was needed and to check up on workers. Foreign firms were hired to undertake those projects that required sophisticated technology. The whole operation was funded by the export of food, government levies and the ruthless expropriation of profits and surpluses by the state.

Good transportation and communications were essential for industrialization. This picture from 1930 shows workers building the railroad from Siberia to Turkestan.

By the time the Second Five-Year Plan was in operation the government had begun to shift its emphasis from force to persuasion. Piecework (work paid for according to the quantity produced) and wage differentials (different rates of pay for different types of work) were introduced. Medals, such as the Order of Lenin, were awarded to outstanding workers. The most famous achievement was that of Alexander Stakhanov, who mined 102 tons of coal in six hours – fourteen times the quota. He was blessed with supportive colleagues and machinery that did not break down. Some would-be "Stakhanovites" died of overwork; others were killed by fellow workers who feared being held to such an inhuman standard.

15

Profit and loss

The First Five-Year Plan and its successors hit the Soviet Union with tremendous impact. The USSR became a great industrial nation; from being the fifth industrial nation when the plans began, it was eventually second only to the United States.[11]

There was a huge increase in Soviet industrial production between 1928 and 1940 as shown in the tables below.

Industrial production in the Soviet Union[12]		
	1928	*1940*
Steel (millions of tonnes)	4	18.3
Coal (millions of tonnes)	31	165.9
Oil (millions of tonnes)	11.7	31.1
Electricity (millions of KWh)	5.1	48.6
Cars (thousands)	0.8	145
Tractors (thousands)	1.3	31.6
(1 tonne = 1.102 tons)		

Two points have to be borne in mind when analyzing these figures. First, as one historian points out, "There are strong grounds for treating Soviet economic production statistics with considerable skepticism."[14] All the factories had to produce a huge quantity of goods, according to strict quotas laid down by the Plans, otherwise the workers, and those in charge, would be punished. This led individual factory managers to exaggerate their production figures.

Second, rapid industrialization did not automatically mean a better life for all Soviet citizens. A large number were forced to move from their villages to new cities, such as Magnitogorsk, where conditions were often appalling. While the output of capital goods rose almost thirteenfold, the production of consumer goods increased only fourfold.[15] Wages in real terms were lower in 1937 than

Production in the major European industrialized countries, 1940*[13]				
	USSR	*UK*	*GERMANY*	*FRANCE*
Coal (millions of tonnes)	165.9	240	360	47
Steel (millions of tonnes)	18.3	13.4	19	4.4
Motor vehicles (thousands)	240	450	345	234
Electricity (millions of KWh)	48.6	30	40	20
(1 tonne = 1.102 tons)				

* Approximations are given where exact comparisons are not available.

.СО ЗНАМЕНЕМ ЛЕНИНА ПОБЕДИЛИ МЫ В БОЯХ ЗА ОКТЯБРЬСКУЮ РЕВОЛЮЦИЮ.
СО ЗНАМЕНЕМ ЛЕНИНА ДОБИЛИСЬ МЫ РЕШАЮЩИХ УСПЕХОВ В БОРЬБЕ ЗА ПОБЕДУ
СОЦИАЛИСТИЧЕСКОГО СТРОИТЕЛЬСТВА.
С ЭТИМ ЖЕ ЗНАМЕНЕМ ПОБЕДИМ В ПРОЛЕТАРСКОЙ РЕВОЛЮЦИИ ВО ВСЕМ МИРЕ·
(Сталин. Политический отчет ЦК XVI съезду ВКП(б).)

The enemy without ... The banner above the factory says that the First Five-Year Plan was achieved despite the opposition of foreign liberals, capitalists and priests.

they had been in 1928.[16] The state became excessively bureaucratic; there was so much paperwork that it was hard for the government to discover the inefficiencies. Output per worker remained comparatively low, and Soviet goods were often shoddy. The industrial achievement of the first three Five-Year Plans was certainly

remarkable, but the average Soviet worker did not profit from it materially.

The enemy within . . . In this poster, which was displayed in factories, a drunken worker tries to hold back the advance of Soviet industry. Workers were urged to write the names of "slackers" (lazy workers) in the space below.

Collectivization

The Five-Year Plans set targets for agriculture as well as for industry. They also changed the way Soviet farming was organized. Peasant holdings were combined to form collective farms (*kolkhozy*) or state farms (*sovkhozy*). In the former, peasants handed over all their resources to the collective, including their land, in return for a share of the profits. In the *sovkhozy* all land and goods were owned by the state, and the laborers worked for wages.

The Party did not announce all the reasons for collectivization. Not all of the following explanations were made public.

- Greater efficiency: ". . . the socialist way . . . is to set up collective and state farms . . . [which can be] technically and scientifically equipped."[17]
- Control of the population: it was much easier for the government to direct the thinking and behavior of the peasants if they were organized into a relatively small number of large collectives.
- The need for capital: industrial expansion had to be financed by the sale of agricultural produce – it has been estimated that the state paid the collectives one-eighth of the market price for their grain. The remaining seven-eighths was invested in industry.[18]
- Ideology: ". . . can it be denied that the collective farms . . . represent . . . a new path of development of the countryside, the socialist path . . . as opposed to the . . . capitalist path?"[19]
- Counteracting the NEP: the government was worried that the NEP's success was undermining socialism by encouraging private gain.

An official Soviet photograph from 1930, showing *kulaks* being forcibly deported from their villages. They have been made to hold a banner reading "Destroy the *Kulak* Class Immediately."

Meal time on a collective farm, 1938. The collective farms changed the peasants' whole way of life, not just the way in which they worked.

Collectivization took place in stages. In 1928–9 the government attempted to force the peasants into collective farms. The *kulaks*, the richer peasants, were to be "eliminated as a class." Sometimes whole villages were destroyed, and there is evidence that grain was deliberately withheld from the peasants who refused to move. *Kulak* became a term of abuse to describe all who resisted collectivization.

By March 1930 fourteen million peasant households were in *kolkhozy*. Faced with famine and massive resistance, however, Stalin was forced to backtrack – two months later only five million households remained in the *kolkhozy*.[20] A new approach involving economic incentives rather than force produced better results: at the end of the First Five-Year Plan 78 percent of all cultivated land was farmed collectively.[21]

By the end of 1937 the process was virtually complete. About twenty-five million small farms had been replaced by a quarter of a million *kolkhozy* and *sovkhozy*.[22]

Rural disaster

The policy of collectivization was a failure economically and a disaster in human terms. This table illustrates how close agricultural production came to the targets set in the Five-Year Plans:

Percentage of goal achieved in First and Second Five-Year Plans[23]		
	1st Plan	2nd Plan
Official Soviet estimate	57.8	62.6–76.9
Estimate of Western economist	50.7	69.0

The Soviet figures, which were certainly inflated, show that agricultural production failed to reach even three-quarters of the expected target.

The next table gives information about specific sectors of agriculture[24]:

This court tried farmers accused of failing to meet production targets.

Official Soviet Production Figures 1928 - 40			
1 tonne = 1.102 tons	1928	1932	1940
Grain (million tonnes)	73.3	69.6	95.6
Sugar (million tonnes)	1.3	0.8	2.2
Number of pigs (million)	22.0	10.9	22.5
Number of cows (million)	29.3	22.3	22.8

The increases in grain and sugar output between 1928 and 1940 are quite impressive. They were commodities that the government needed to sell to finance industrial development. In the second phase of collectivization (from 1930) the peasants did not have to hand over all their resources to the *kolkhoz*, but were permitted to keep small plots of land for their own private use. This might help to explain the decline in sugar production between 1928 and 1932, and the subsequent sharp rise in production. The decrease in the number of cows and pigs between 1928 and 1932 is also significant; when forced collectivization was first introduced many peasants killed their livestock rather than hand it over to a *kolkhoz*. The number of farm animals, including horses used for drawing machinery, fell by at least half between 1929 and 1933.[25]

The collective farms proved generally to be inefficient. The peasants were used to farming their own plots of land for their food and selling any surplus to make a profit. But all the surplus from the collective farms was taken by the government and was used to

РАБОЧЕГО СНАБЖЕНИЯ

feed the urban workers. So the peasants did not directly benefit from their work. The motivation to produce more was lost.

The human effects of the collectivization policy were twofold. First, a terrible famine in 1932–3 killed an estimated five million people.[26] Second, Stalin's aim of "squeezing out the capitalist elements in the rural districts," in other words the *kulaks*, was ruthlessly carried out.[27] Two and a half million families, perhaps twelve million

A Soviet propaganda poster entitled "Down with Those who Keep Food from the Workers." The government refused to accept responsibility for shortages, and instead blamed the peasants for hoarding food.

people, simply disappeared. Some were shot, some starved to death, others were deported to labor camps in remote parts of the USSR. The effort to "eliminate the *kulaks* as a class" had succeeded.[28]

21

3
STALINISM
Communism

KARL MARX, the father of modern communism, stated that history moved through identifiable stages: from feudalism, to capitalism, and finally (he predicted) to socialism. He said that this last transition would begin with the revolution of the working classes against their masters. Then would follow a period known as the "dictatorship of the proletariat" (or working classes), when capitalist ways and thinking would be eliminated. Eventually, a stateless socialist world would emerge, without classes or private property, "in which the free development of each is the condition for the free development of all."[29]

Following the revolution of November 1917, the Russian Communist Party believed that it was entering the stage of the dictatorship of the proletariat. Certain conditions would have to be fulfilled to create a fair and classless society. It is interesting to compare the aims of the Bolsheviks in 1917 with Stalin's policies:

1 Industrialization. The Bolsheviks believed that industrialization was necessary to satisfy the material needs of the socialist society. Stalin introduced a series of Five-Year Plans.
2 Spreading the revolution to other nations. Stalin adopted a policy of "socialism in one country."
3 Weeding out all members of the bourgeoisie (ruling class) and ensuring that capitalist ideas did not creep back into Soviet society. In 1934 Stalin declared:

> . . . we are heading for the formation of a classless socialist society. It goes without saying that [this] . . . cannot come of itself . . . It has to be . . . built by the efforts of all the working people, by strengthening the organs of the dictatorship of the proletariat [particularly the Party], by intensifying the class struggle, by abolishing classes, by eliminating the remnants of the capitalist classes, and in battle with enemies both internal and external.[30]

Many class differences were eliminated by the Bolshevik revolution. Later, under Stalin, most people in the cities earned roughly the same wages and lived in similar houses. However, the Party officials benefited from

Women were granted equal status to men following the Bolshevik revolution. The facilities portrayed in this propaganda poster enable women to participate more fully in the labor force.

Karl Marx.

huge privileges denied to other citizens. Stalin, in fact, created a new kind of privileged class.

Today, most people are skeptical about the possibility of creating a classless society, especially people in eastern Europe and the Soviet Union who have lived through what has been called socialism. Important questions in the debate are whether every socialist revolution would lead to a dictator- ship, and whether power corrupts all those who hold it, however well-meaning they may be.

The purges

The Russian word *chistika* means "a purification." "Purge," the English translation, fails to capture the sinister import of the word as Stalin used it; "massacre" would be a more accurate alternative. From 1934 on, Stalin used a series of purges to eliminate anyone who might oppose him.

Although Stalin was unquestionably the most powerful single figure in the USSR after 1929, there were still those within the Party who challenged some of his actions. In 1932 Stalin's second wife committed suicide partly in reaction to the cruelties of collectivization. In the same year the Politburo gave a comparatively lenient punishment to M. N. Ryutin and his supporters for their sweeping condemnation of Stalin, "the evil genius of the Russian revolution."[31] This encouraged the opposition to Stalin, which was focused around Sergei Kirov, the Leningrad Party Secretary. But Kirov was assassinated in December 1934, clearly on Stalin's instructions, and the Leningrad Party was purged of his supporters. Several thousand people were deported to Siberia. Stalin was to use the NKVD (as the secret police was now known) to eliminate systematically millions of citizens.

One historian has written: "It would be almost impossible to exaggerate the sufferings of the Soviet people during this period."[31] The public face of the massacre was three show trials (August 1936, January–February 1937 and March 1938) in which all Stalin's old Bolshevik colleagues – Zinoviev, Kamenev, Bukharin and Rykov among them – were found guilty of trumped-up charges. They were either executed or sent to labor camps and certain death. Trotsky, in exile in Mexico, was murdered with an alpenstock by Stalin's agents in 1940. Almost all the Central Committee of the Party, most high-ranking army officers, and countless diplomats, engineers, scientists and government officials died in the purges, as did many thousands of other ordinary people.

Before long the terror acquired a momentum of its own. The following telegram was sent in 1937:

> *To NKVD, Frunze. You are charged with exterminating 10,000 enemies of the people. Report results by signal. YEZHOV.* [33]

The exiled Leon Trotsky, seen here with his wife, Natalya, in Denmark in 1932, continued his revolutionary work abroad. In his writings he attacked Stalin for betraying the Bolshevik revolution, and advocated strategies for the communist parties around the world to follow.

▲ In this illustration in an Italian fascist magazine from 1937, Party members invited to the Kremlin to meet Stalin are arrested.

Nikolai Yezhov, head of the NKVD since September 1936, was demanding 10,000 more deaths, just to demonstrate that he was doing his job well.

Stalin dismissed all criticism of the purges:

> Foreigners have been talking drivel to the effect that the purging . . . of spies, assassins and wreckers . . . has "shaken" the Soviet system . . .[34]

Estimates of the labor camp population at the end of the 1930s vary from three to fifteen million, and the numbers who died as a result of Stalin's purges are at least as great – perhaps twenty million people.[35] The dream of 1917 had become a nightmare.

▼A local purge committee at work in 1933 weeding out Party members who were suspected of activity against the Soviet state.

New conservatism

The Bolshevik revolution, in changing the social system in Russia, heralded a wave of radicalism and experimentation that extended to every sphere of life, from the role of women and attitudes toward religion, to the arts. As a response to the repression of the 1930s the Soviet people became deeply conservative. Many of the radical developments that had been ushered in by the revolution were rejected in favor of traditional customs. The Stalinist state adopted many features of the old Czarist system, such as a huge bureaucracy and a new emphasis on the power of the state. Ranks in the Army, abolished after the revolution, were reintroduced, and officers' privileges were reinstated.

For most of the 1920s the USSR had been led by intellectuals, trained in law or the humanities. During the next decade a new class of leader emerged, mostly of peasant stock. They graduated in technical subjects and rose rapidly in industry, the Party and the government, taking over the jobs of the old Bolsheviks who had retired or been purged. These upwardly-mobile young men, who included the future Soviet premiers Nikita Khrushchev and Leonid Brezhnev, did not wish to change a system that had benefited them. Many were still in power in the 1980s. They adopted the tastes and styles of the old bourgeoisie, wearing fashionable suits and patronizing the unimaginative but impressive architecture, such as the Moscow University building (opened in 1953).

The Soviet government placed great emphasis on education. Indeed, the advance of educational standards throughout the

Five marshals of the Red Army in the mid-1930s, after the reintroduction of ranks into the Army.

Moscow State University, one of the most famous monuments to the Stalinist era.

country was one of its outstanding achievements. About 85 percent of the population was literate by 1941, compared with just over 50 percent fifteen years earlier. The state provided a network of elementary schools, and all urban centers had a secondary school.[36] By 1955 over one and a half million students were in higher education; the figure for 1910 was 40,000.[37] But under Stalin the curriculum became more traditional, recognizing national heroes from the Czarist era, such as Peter the Great, who had been reviled by the Bolsheviks. Also, single-sex schools were reintroduced.

After 1917 divorce and abortion had been made freely available, and women gained more control over their own lives. Stalin's government reversed this doctrine. Wedding rings became available once more, divorce was made expensive, and the concept of illegitimate children was reintroduced. This was the official propaganda:

> *The state cannot exist without the family. Marriage has a positive value for the Soviet socialist state only if the partners see in it a lifelong union. So-called "free love" is a bourgeois invention . . .*[38]

Stalin saw that there was a link between discipline and control in the home and control of society as a whole. The regime reinforced the new conservatism of the people for its own ends.

Totalitarianism

Totalitarianism is a form of government that emerged in various countries during the first half of the twentieth century. The term originated in Italy to describe the Fascist regime of Benito Mussolini. It has also been applied to Hitler's Germany and the Soviet Union under Stalin. These are the basic features of a totalitarian regime:

1 Central control of the economy by the state.
2 Only one political party allowed to exist.
3 State-controlled media.
4 A ruthless secret police.
5 A god-like national figurehead.
6 An official ideology, which takes priority over the law, religion and individual conscience.[39]

Although the USSR undoubtedly became totalitarian under Stalin, the dictator never openly acknowledged the fact. The state comprised a number of separate republics, embracing a wide diversity of individual races, cultures and religions. Personal freedoms were in theory guaranteed by the new constitution that Stalin introduced in 1936. He called it "the only thoroughly democratic Constitution in the world."[40] (Ironically, several of the authors of the new constitution, such as Bukharin, perished in the purges.) The constitution reorganized the system of government, allowed all adults to vote and guaranteed freedom of speech, the press, assembly and religious worship. But what happened in practice suggests that the constitution was seldom invoked.

• Of the 163 Christian bishops active in 1930, only 12 were still at liberty in 1939.[41]

An illustration in an Italian fascist magazine from 1932, showing Russian Christians being burned to death in a barn in which they had been holding a service.

Stalin – head of state, head of the Party and head of the Comintern – is mocked as the "Soviet Trinity" in this cartoon, 1936. By this date his power within the USSR was virtually unchallenged.

- In 1912 there were 26,279 mosques in Russia; in 1942 there were only 1,312.[42]
- The author of this poem, Oslip Mandelstam, was arrested for writing it and eventually died in a labor camp:

> *We live, deaf to the land beneath us,*
> *Ten steps away no one hears our speeches,*
> *All we hear is the Kremlin mountaineer,*
> *The murderer and the peasant slayer.*
> *His fingers are fat as grubs*
> *And the words, final as lead weights, fall from*
> *   his lips,*
> *His cockroach whiskers leer*
> *And his boot-tops gleam.*[43]

Stalin forbade opposition parties, stating:

> *As to freedom for various political parties . . .*
> *there is no ground in the USSR for the existence*
> *of several parties, and . . . for freedom for those*
> *parties . . . In the USSR only one party can*
> *exist, the Communist Party.*[44]

According to one historian, the result of the huge disparity between Stalinist theory and practice was that

> *. . . probably the majority of the population could*
> *not believe the official ideology. [They] . . . were*
> *compelled to live two . . . lives, a public one*
> *where they repeated the grotesque falsehoods . . .*
> *and a private one . . . where perhaps the truth*
> *was faced, if one had the courage to face it.*[45]

4
THE USSR AND THE WORLD
Settling down

IT TOOK SEVERAL YEARS for the revolutionary Bolshevik regime to become accepted internationally, owing to strong misgivings on both sides. The communists believed that workers all over the world had more in common with each other than with the bourgeoisie of their own countries. The *Communist Manifesto* had ended with the ringing cry: "Workers Of All Countries, Unite!"

The Bolsheviks hoped that the revolution would spread to other countries to create a world communist system, in which national boundaries would become irrelevant. So the new communist government did not pursue diplomatic relations with the capitalist states. Not surprisingly, for some time the Western nations regarded Soviet Russia as a monster that ought to be strangled at birth: not only did it advocate world revolution, but it also refused to repay the Czarist regime's debts.

In 1919 the Bolsheviks founded the Third International, known as the Comintern, to foment socialist revolution internationally. The communist parties around the world followed the political line dictated by the USSR, thus undermining the official policies of their own governments.

By 1922, however, the situation had changed. First, the Soviet government was preoccupied with internal problems, so it was not in a position to threaten other states. Second, the revolution had failed to spread beyond the borders of the USSR, and was unlikely to do so in the near future. So the way was clear for the Commissar for Foreign Affairs, Georgi Chicherin, to try to establish more friendly relations with other countries.

In 1922 Germany and the Soviet Union were international outcasts. It was not surprising, therefore, that they settled their differences

Czechoslovakian troops occupy the Russian city of Irkutsk during the civil war, 1918. The Czech Army was one of the many foreign armies that invaded Russia after the revolution.

The Chinese nationalist leader Chiang Kai-shek (on horseback). In 1925–7 he defeated the communist guerrillas in China. If the latter had won, the USSR would no longer have been isolated, and communism around the world might have been strengthened.

and by the Treaty of Rapallo established full diplomatic relations. Claims for war reparations were dropped and steps were taken to increase trade between the two countries. The Russians also permitted the Germans to use Soviet soil to develop weapons forbidden to them by the post-World War II Treaty of Versailles. Two years later ten other countries formally recognized the USSR. They included Britain, France, Italy and China, but not the United States.

The USSR's international position improved following Stalin's seizure of power and the adoption of the doctrine of "socialism in one country." Though Stalin would periodically warn that "things are heading for a new war," and he still talked of the inevitable clash between socialism and capitalism, his attitude toward the Western nations was not openly aggressive:

> Our foreign policy is . . . a policy of preserving peace and of strengthening commercial relations with all countries.[46]

The governments of other countries were reassured by Stalin's doctrine of "socialism in one country" rather than world revolution.

The Bolsheviks of 1917 would never have agreed with Stalin's policy of seeking friendly relations with the capitalist countries.

The search for security

In 1922 the Fascist leader Mussolini became head of state in Italy. For many years, however, the Soviet government did not take the fascist movement in Europe seriously, believing it to be merely a militant version of capitalism. A series of events in the 1930s forced the USSR to change its policy:

- Japan, whose leaders had fascist sympathies, invaded mainland China in 1931.
- Hitler seized power in Germany in 1933 and promptly liquidated the German Communist Party.
- The fascist movement was growing in Spain.

After 1933 Stalin needed not just friends outside the Soviet Union, but allies.

In 1934 the USSR joined the League of Nations and made ten-year defense agreements with the Baltic States (Latvia, Estonia and Lithuania) and with Poland. The following year it signed treaties with Czechoslovakia and France, and sent aid to the Nationalists in China to help them fight the Japanese. The Comintern called in vain for an international alliance against fascism. In 1936 Germany and Japan responded by signing an Anti-Comintern Pact, joined by Italy in 1937 and Spain in 1939.

In 1936 the Western countries were presented with two opportunities to thwart fascist expansion, when German troops reoccupied the demilitarized Rhineland, and when a military coup plunged Spain into civil war. But Britain and France merely looked on disapprovingly and did not respond. It seemed to the Soviet Union that the capitalist states were hoping that fascism might eliminate communism for them. These fears increased considerably after the 1938 Munich Conference, at which Britain and France refused to stop Hitler from occupying Czechoslovakia, which was close to the USSR.

Germans in Czechoslovakian Sudetenland showing their support for the Nazis, 1938.

НАСТУПАЕТ

'АЗДАВИМ ГАДИНУ
МОЩНЫМ КОНТРНАСТУПЛЕНИЕМ

A Soviet anti-Nazi poster, 1930.

By 1939 Stalin had two choices:

1 Try to reach an agreement with the West to resist Germany, a difficult task considering the West's suspicious and hostile attitude toward the Soviet Union.

2 Come to an agreement with Hitler.

He chose the latter, and on August 23, 1939, the Nazi–Soviet Non-Aggression Pact was signed. Secret clauses divided Poland between the two powers and accepted the future Soviet annexation of Finland and the Baltic States.

Some Western historians saw the signing of the pact by Stalin as a cynical act of appeasement that unleashed World War II. A Soviet scholar is less critical:

> ... the nonaggression pact should not be added to ... Stalin's [list of] errors and crimes. The Soviet government was compelled to sign the pact because Britain and France had been encouraging German Fascism, and were frustrating the negotiations for a mutual assistance pact with the Soviet Union ... [This] compelled the Soviet Union to protect itself.[47]

World War II

The Non-Aggression Pact of August 1939 did not bring lasting peace for the Soviet Union, but it did buy the country time. On June 22, 1941, Hitler launched Operation Barbarossa: a German force of some 3.2 million men invaded the USSR along a broad front. Although individual units of the Red Army put up brave resistance, the Nazis advanced swiftly toward Moscow and Leningrad. The Germans knew that they could not hope to defeat the USSR in a prolonged war and that the country was too vast for them to occupy. Their plan, therefore, was to use "blitzkrieg" (lightning war) tactics: attacking swiftly in great strength, surrounding enemy divisions and forcing them to surrender. They believed that after a few crushing defeats either the Soviet leaders would sue for peace or the country would break up into its constituent republics. These could then be assimilated into the German Empire.

The German plan almost succeeded. After a diversion toward the rich farmlands and

In 1941–2 the Red Army pursued a "scorched earth" policy, destroying everything that might have been of use to the German invaders. These people in a Nazi-occupied village are searching for food in a garbage dump.

oilfields of the south, on September 30, Hitler ordered Operation Typhoon – an all-out assault on Moscow. Stalin panicked and left the capital for a night. Citizens tore up their Party cards and prepared to accept occupation. But the Nazis failed to occupy Moscow. In December 1941 they were driven back from the capital, largely owing to the fine leadership of Marshal Zhukov and the arrival of fresh troops and supplies from the east.

The Germans advanced again in 1942, this time to Stalingrad on the Volga River. Once more they were met by huge resistance. When winter came the ill-prepared Germans suffered terribly from the icy conditions, and in January 1943 Field Marshal Von Paulus and the bedraggled remnants of his Sixth Army finally surrendered. Soviet morale soared. The Soviet Army had defeated the Germans in battle for the first time. Further Soviet victories soon followed, notably in the tank

A woman tractor driver in Daghestan (on the northern side of the Caucasus mountains) receiving lessons in rifle firing, mid-1942. The people of Daghestan were learning guerrilla warfare tactics, to be used if the Nazis invaded.

battle waged at Kursk in June–July 1943. After this the Russians moved on to the offensive and began to advance toward Berlin, the capital of Germany.

The Red Army advanced steadily westward throughout 1944. Not only did it push toward Germany, it also marched into Czechoslovakia, Romania, Bulgaria and Yugoslavia. Soviet troops entered Warsaw in January 1945, Vienna three months later, and finally took Berlin in May. By the end of World War II the USSR had proved itself to be a superpower, although the cost of victory had been extremely high. The implications of this military success for the future were enormous.

Soviet victory

The news of the German attack in June 1941 came as such a shock to Stalin that for eight days he remained in his country residence, cut off from the rest of the country and, some said, drinking heavily. He believed that the end had come.

Stalin was responsible for failing to foresee Operation Barbarossa. For more than ten years Hitler had made it quite clear that he thought the Slav races were inferior, fit only for slavery. At the same time Stalin had continually urged the USSR to strengthen itself against possible capitalist aggression. Moreover, for months before, spies and British intelligence had warned him that an invasion was imminent. Stalin's faith in the Non-Aggression Pact is difficult to comprehend.

The Soviet victory over the German Army in 1941 was unexpected, considering the ease with which the German Army had swept through Europe. Despite the rise of fascism

Stalin's authority in the USSR was boosted by the Soviet victory in 1945.

A Soviet poster of 1942, promoting the alliance against the fascist governments. Considering what they had been told about the West in previous years, the citizens of the USSR must have been surprised to see posters like this.

in the Western countries in the 1930s and the growing threat of war, the USSR had been ill-prepared for attack, and most of the Army's experienced commanders had fallen victim to the purges.

The part played by Stalin in the Soviet victory is difficult to assess. He panicked at crucial moments and had little ability as a strategic commander. Yet he was an important focus for his people's resistance, and his stirring speech on July 3, 1941, when he announced the invasion and urged everyone to "defend every inch of Soviet soil . . . fight to the last drop of blood," rallied the nation.

Other explanations for Soviet success include:
- The alienating effect of German brutality – 3.3 million Soviet prisoners died in captivity.[48]
- The skill of commanders such as Zhukov.
- Supplies sent to the USSR from the West.
- Soviet superiority in arms production and in the design of some weapons (especially tanks and rockets).
- German strategic blunders, their ill-preparedness for winter campaigns, and the fact that the USSR was not their only battle front.
- The USSR's huge reserves of labor.

5
THE FINAL PHASE
Recovery

IN 1945 a Western visitor to the USSR wrote:

> For thousands of miles there was not a standing
> or living object to be seen. Every town was flat,
> every city. There were no barns, no machinery,
> no stations. There was not a single telegraph
> pole left standing . . . The houses all being gone,
> the people were living in dug-outs; pits dug into
> the earth, and roofed over with fir branches,
> wattle and earth. [49]

**War damage in the Soviet Republic of Latvia,
1945. The devastation in the western USSR
was far greater than that suffered by Britain or
France.**

As a result of the war the USSR lost:

- **14-20 million people**
- **4.7 million homes**
- **1,700 towns**
- **70,000 villages**
- **98,000 *kolkhozy***
- **1,876 *sovkhozy***
- **31,000 factories**
- **40,000 miles of railroad**
- **1,300 bridges**
- **137,000 tractors**
- **7 million horses**
- **17 million head of cattle**
- **20 million pigs**

One quarter of the country's wealth may have
been destroyed.[50]

A modern coal mine in the Kemerovo region of the USSR, 1953. By this date the economy had fully recovered from the destruction caused by World War II, and industrial production exceeded pre-1941 levels.

Soviet economists introduced new Five-Year Plans in an attempt to repair the damage caused by the war. As the table below shows, the Fourth and Fifth Five-Year Plans (1946–50 and 1950–55) produced remarkable results. The 1940 and 1945 figures give some indication of the level of wartime destruction, although it has been suggested that the 1945 statistics shown here may be lower than the true figures.

Although real wages were still lower in 1950 than before the war, and the success of the Plans was exaggerated by using questionable accounting methods, the Soviet achievement was considerable.[52] The Soviet economy was now the second most powerful in the world. The USSR had acquired a huge empire in eastern Europe with which it could trade on favorable terms. Its wealth enabled it to support communist regimes in other parts of the world, particularly in China, and great advances were made in technology as well as in basic industries. The Soviet Union exploded its first atomic bomb in 1949. Eight years later, to the amazement of the West, it launched the first space satellite, Sputnik 1.

Industrial and agricultural production figures[51]

	1940	1945	1950	1960
Steel (millions of tonnes)	18.3	12.3	27.3	65.3
Coal (millions of tonnes)	165.9	49.3	261.1	510
Oil (millions of tonnes)	31.1	19.4	37.9	148
Tractors (thousands)	31.6	14.7	109	239
Grain (millions of tonnes)	95.6	47.3	81.2	126
Sugar (millions of tonnes)	2.2	0.5	2.5	6.4

(1 tonne = 1.102 tons)

An ageing dictator

In 1947 a group of Soviet historians published a biography of Stalin. This excerpt illustrates the extreme to which the "cult" of Stalin was taken. It was simply not possible at that time to write a biography of Stalin that was less than extravagantly complimentary.

Stalin is the brilliant leader and teacher of the Party, the great strategist of the Socialist Revolution, military commander, and guide of the Soviet state . . . Everybody is familiar with the cogent and invincible force of Stalin's logic, the crystal clarity of his mind, his iron will, his devotion to the Party, his ardent faith in the people, and love for the people. Everybody is familiar with his modesty, his simplicity of manner, his consideration for people, and his merciless severity towards enemies of the people.[53]

Stalin carefully created a mysterious image. He traveled little, and when he appeared in public he usually stood on a tall rostrum to disguise his small five-foot-three stature. In photographs his hair was not shown as white as it really was, and the pockmarks on his face were skillfully painted out. The real Stalin was "an old small man, with a face ravaged by the years."[54] He became increasingly fearful and suspicious with age. Nikolai Bulganin, a Soviet prime minister in the 1950s, recalled:

It happens sometimes that a man goes to Stalin, invited as a friend; and when he sits with Stalin he does not know where he will be sent next, home or to jail.[55]

A stylized Soviet painting of Stalin giving a speech in the 1930s. After 1945 the Stalin cult reached new heights in the Soviet Union, and such pictures were displayed in most public places.

A statue of Stalin in Czechoslovakia, photographed in 1989 after the collapse of the Czech communist government. The statue was a gaunt reminder of Soviet dominance in eastern Europe for forty years after the end of World War II.

Khrushchev was equally critical:

> *Stalin was a very distrustful man, diseased with suspicion . . . He could look at you and say: "Why are your eyes so shifty today?" And after the war he became even more capricious, irritable, and brutal . . . His persecution mania reached unbelievable dimensions.*[56]

At home in his *dacha* Stalin fed song-birds, played billiards, listened to music and tended his garden with loving care. But while one minute he could be pruning his roses, the next he could be ordering the extermination of thousands of Soviet citizens. Such was the paranoid personality of the ruler of one of the most powerful nations on earth.

41

The unchanging regime

Stalin's totalitarian regime continued after 1945. Stalin maintained an iron grip on the Party and all organizations of government, although he often had little idea of what was really going on in the country. Officials were so afraid of Stalin that they gave him only the news he wished to hear. When told of something displeasing, he usually rejected it as lies or announced that it was the result of some counter-revolutionary conspiracy – in which case those responsible had to be hunted down and either executed or sent to labor camps.

An extraordinary example of Stalin's paranoia was the treatment meted out to Soviet soldiers who had been captured by the Nazis during World War II. When they returned to the Soviet Union after the war they were not permitted to see their relatives or to rejoin the Army. The soldiers were interrogated and sent to prison camps, branded as traitors. Their "crime" was to have disobeyed Stalin's order never to be captured alive by the enemy. Many civilians from areas that had been occupied by the Nazis were treated similarly.

The Party continued to grow and dominate all aspects of Soviet life. The best jobs were reserved for its members and its machinery was used to vet all prominent figures, from factory managers to concert pianists. As one might expect, intellectual and cultural life reached a new level of sterility.

Stalin insisted on viewing all new Soviet movies. Composers whose work had previously been widely appreciated, such as Shostakovich, now fell from favor. The dictator encouraged this atmosphere of absolute fear and mistrust quite deliberately. As long as no one dared trust anyone else, and as long as he was the supreme arbiter of everything, from painting to potato-growing, he felt safe.

The rights of women and non-Russians within the USSR were further suppressed during the final phase of Stalin's rule. Women

Collective Farm on Holiday, **painted by S.V. Gerasimov, 1937. Pictures like this won high praise from the Soviet authorities.**

who had filled men's jobs during the war were now forced out of work by the returning soldiers. The law no longer held men responsible for their illegitimate children; Stalin personally pardoned a soldier for shooting a colleague who had tried to prevent him from raping a woman. In May 1945 Stalin proposed a toast to "the Russian people because it is the most eminent of all the nations belonging to the Soviet Union."[57] The speech heralded a period of lavish praise for all things Russian, at the expense of other

Dimitri Shostakovich, one of the leading Soviet composers of the Stalinist era. He frequently found himself torn between writing the kind of music he wanted to write and producing work to please the government.

Soviet peoples, particularly Jews. The Jewish State Theater in Moscow was closed in 1949, and the next year Stalin declared Russian to be the only true proletarian language. Stalin had long since rejected his own Georgian background.

Superpower

Following the defeat of Germany, Japan and Italy in World War II, and the severe weakening of Britain and France, the United States and the USSR emerged as the superpowers of the modern world. At the Yalta and Potsdam peace conferences in 1945, the USSR, Britain and the United States attempted to agree upon the political frontiers of the post-war world. But the conflicts of interest between them soon became apparent. The American possession of the A-bomb, successfully detonated over Hiroshima and Nagasaki in August 1945, increased the tension. The Soviet Union consequently made moves to extend its control over the countries of eastern Europe, which it had liberated at the end of the war.

In 1947 the USSR established friendly "satellite" governments in Hungary, Poland, Bulgaria, Romania and (in 1948) in Czechoslovakia. The eastern part of Germany became the German Democratic Republic in 1949. Soviet-style governments and secret police systems were introduced into the Soviet bloc countries, and in 1949 the Council for Mutual Economic Assistance (Comecon) was formed to link them economically. Contact with the West was greatly reduced, as an "iron curtain" fell across Europe. This was the beginning of what became known as the Cold War.

The Soviet Union regarded the establishment of satellite states in eastern Europe as a defensive measure, to protect itself from the West. In the century and a half before 1945 Russia had been invaded three times (1812, 1914–18 and 1941–44), and on each occasion had suffered appalling devastation. By 1946 the USSR was determined that this should never happen again.

The United States saw the creation of the Soviet bloc as an act of communist aggression, and President Truman responded in 1947 with this doctrine:

> I believe that it must be the policy of the United States to support free peoples who are resisting attempted subjugation by armed minorities or by outside pressures . . . I believe that our help should be primarily through economic and financial aid . . .[58]

Truman saw that the economies of western Europe were very weak, so the European Recovery Program, or Marshall Plan, was developed to help these countries with U.S. economic aid. Under the Marshall Plan aid was offered to all the European states, but Stalin naturally refused to allow the capitalists to interfere in eastern Europe.

A Chinese propaganda picture entitled *Children's Heroes*, 1951. The children are holding placards showing Mao Zedong, the Chinese leader, and Stalin. After the Chinese communist revolution in 1949, the USSR and China became allies.

A map showing the division of Europe after World War II. Many of the western European countries joined NATO in response to the creation of the Soviet bloc.

Through this program the United States extended its economic influence in western Europe.

The Cold War spread to Asia following the communist revolution in China in 1949. In 1950 Soviet-backed North Korea invaded U.S.-backed South Korea. The United States saw this as further evidence of the increasing threat of world communism and invaded Korea. In 1949 the United States set up NATO, the first of several international alliances formed to "contain" the Soviet Union by surrounding it with military bases.

For the next forty years the Cold War between the superpowers dominated world politics.

6
THE END OF THE REGIME
A fallen hero

A T ABOUT 4 a.m. on March 6, 1953, broadcasting on the Soviet state radio was interrupted by a roll of drums. When it was over the solemn voice of an announcer uttered the following words:

> . . . the heart of the comrade-in-arms . . . the wise leader and teacher of the Communist Party and the Soviet Union, has ceased to beat. [59]

Stalin was dead.

Many ordinary Soviet citizens could hardly believe their ears. They could not imagine life without Stalin. He had dominated the country, in peace and war, for

Long lines of people waiting to see Stalin's body as it lay in state in Moscow's Hall of Columns, 1953. Eighteen years later the dictator's body was removed from its place of honor beside that of Lenin and was buried in a simple grave near the wall of the Kremlin.

Hungarian rebels on a tank captured from the Soviet Army, waving the Hungarian national flag, 1956. Many east Europeans had hoped that the USSR would relax its iron grip on their countries after Stalin's death. But the Hungarian uprising against communist rule in 1956 was rapidly crushed by the Red Army. It was not until 1989 that the communist government was overthrown in Hungary.

twenty-six years. A whole generation had grown up knowing no other leader. At school, on the radio and in the work-place he had consistently been built up into a god-like figure. It did not seem possible that he was mortal. All over the country the people mourned, even in the labor camps, and they lined up to see Stalin's body as it lay in state in Red Square. Hundreds of people were crushed to death when the crowd got out of control. Even when dead, it seemed, the Man of Steel still had the power to kill his people. His body was embalmed and placed beside that of Lenin in the specially-constructed mausoleum outside the Kremlin.

Stalin's remains did not rest in peace. Eight years later they were removed from their exalted position because it was considered

... inappropriate, since the serious violations by Stalin of Lenin's precepts, abuse of power, mass repressions against honorable Soviet people, and other activities in the period of the personality cult make it impossible to leave the bier with his body in the mausoleum of V. I. Lenin.[60]

The process of "destalinization" began. The new Soviet leader, Nikita Khrushchev, denounced the "personality cult" of Stalin in a secret speech to the Communist Party Congress in 1956. Portraits of the dictator were removed from prominent positions, and before long Soviet historians were permitted to criticize the cruelties and errors of the Stalinist era. Destalinization affected the Soviet satellite states too. In 1956 there were uprisings in Hungary and Poland against communist rule.

However, it was neither a politician nor a historian who portrayed most vividly what the Soviet people had been through. In November 1962 Alexander Solzhenitsyn, who had spent eight years in labor camps for allegedly making derogatory remarks about Stalin, published an account of life in the *Gulag. One Day in the Life of Ivan Denisovich* sold out immediately and became an international best-seller. But it was not until the late 1980s, when Soviet President Gorbachev introduced the policy of *glasnost* (openness), that Western journalists and TV crews were permitted for the first time to speak to Soviet citizens about the Stalinist era.

Stalin on trial

How is it possible to evaluate Stalin's role in Soviet history? While almost no one would deny that he perpetrated many hideous crimes, he was also responsible for many notable achievements. The key question is, in the words of Roy Medvedev, "Which were greater, Stalin's accomplishments or crimes?"[61] Two points of view are set out below.

The Case for the Prosecution:
1 Stalin was a power-crazed dictator, who cared nothing for people and little for the country he governed.

2 He ushered in an inefficient economic system, which relied on force and stamped out individual freedoms.
3 His policies were responsible for perhaps as many as forty million deaths, through famine or deliberate murder.
4 There was some economic and social progress in the USSR under Stalin, but the price was unacceptably high in human terms.

A family living in a basement, Moscow, 1930. The creation of a modern industrial economy took priority over the improvement of workers' living conditions.

ILLUSTRATED—May 1, 1948

The gardens of Moscow University, 1948. Visitors to Moscow saw the outward symbols of wealth, which belied the poor living conditions of the majority of the people as seen in the picture on page 48.

The Case for the Defense:

1 Stalin's Five-Year Plans revolutionized the USSR, turning it into a leading economic power. Between 1928 and 1950 Soviet industrial output increased almost eighteenfold, and living standards rose as well.[62]

2 By 1953 the Soviet people received considerably better education, housing and medical care than they had in 1928.

3 The Soviet defeat of Nazi Germany was made possible by the USSR's technological and industrial development between 1928 and 1941. Stalin also inspired the country's resistance. By 1953 the Soviet state was stronger than it had ever been, and better able to resist any external threat.

Two other arguments have been raised in Stalin's defense.

• Russia had always been an absolutist state and therefore it is possible that only central direction and coercion could have succeeded in modernizing the USSR.

• The West must accept some responsibility for what happened under Stalin. If the Western nations had been less eager to put down the great socialist experiment, Stalin might not have felt so beleaguered, and might then have been less paranoid.

History's verdict

Most historians are deeply critical of Stalin. To Roy Medvedev the man who was "personally responsible for the deaths of many millions of Soviet people, [was] one of the greatest criminals in human history."[63] Robert Payne is even less detached:

> *Like the Pharaohs he murdered with shining impartiality and gave men nothing to live by except mindless obedience. Ruthless almost beyond belief, he killed millions, but this was not his greatest crime. His greatest crime was that he poisoned the sources of Russian life for an entire generation . . . He did not believe in Marx or Lenin; he had no belief in the destiny of the people he ruled; he cared only for his own aggrandizement.[64]*

Other scholars refuse to place Stalin in the same category as Hitler, whose rule brought only destruction. Isaac Deutscher believed that Stalin was "both the leader and the exploiter of a tragic, self-contradictory, but creative revolution."[65] He argued that, harsh and tragic as it was, a Stalinist phase of Soviet development was bound to come about after Lenin's death, whether led by Stalin himself or some other leader. Thus Stalin was a mere tool of history. This "determinist" point of view denies the importance of individual characters in shaping history. It believes that impersonal forces, primarily the economic system, dictate the way societies develop, and that there is no such thing as a "great" man or woman who decides the fate of nations.

Determinists do not believe that Stalin was a particularly talented man. Martin McCauley, on the other hand, argues:

> *It is my belief that Stalin was a very skilled, indeed gifted, politician, and one of the great political figures of the twentieth century. [But] . . . this does not mean that he was a good man. He had a dark, even evil side to his nature.[66]*

What will history's verdict be? Was Stalin a

Children at a collective farm school in Uzbekistan, 1935. Stalin's government brought great achievements in the field of education, particularly in the sciences.

WORLD WIDE SPECIAL

The horror in Stalin's secret killing fields

Stalin: Millions died in his reign of terror

Picture by ALEXANDER CHUNOSOV

BENEATH the shocked gaze of Soviet soldiers, a grim secret of Russia's blood-stained past is revealed.

In this unmarked grave lay the bullet-riddled remains of 356 victims of Stalin's reign of terror in the Thirties.

They were unearthed by the soldiers digging around a disused goldmine in Chelyabinsk in the Ural mountains in central Russia. In the days before glasnost, news of the discovery would have been ruthlessly and swiftly suppressed.

Campaigning

But this and other pictures of the exhumation, taken by investigative journalist Alexander Chunosov, are in an exhibition of his work in a London gallery.

The victims' remains will be officially handed over by the authorities today to surviving relatives for burial, following campaigning by a little-known Soviet organisation called Memorial.

The remains, piled two deep, were found in June and the initial reaction of some Soviet officials was to try to cover up the truth, suggesting that the men and women had starved.

When challenged to explain the bullet holes in the skulls, they were forced to admit that the bones belonged to some of the estimated 80,000 peasant farmers or kulaks slaughtered in the area during a ten-year purge.

In all, about 30 million Soviet citizens, including kulaks, intellectuals, technical specialists, party officials, military personnel, and 'bourgeois nationalists', are

Troops find farmers' mass grave

resisting the state takeover of their farms. They were marched in their thousands from all parts of Russia and assembled at railway stations before being shipped East to isolated labour camps and to new settlements in Soviet Asia. Thanks to perestroika and

police and summarily executed without having a chance to plead their innocence. We had enormous problems getting the authorities to admit they were Kulaks murdered by the secret police.

finding the truth. Supporters of Memorial are pressing the KGB to open files on the terror and plan to resume the search for more of Stalin's killing fields next spring.

Major finds have already been

An article in the British *Daily Mail*, 1989. The true horrors of life under Stalin began to be discussed openly in the USSR in the late 1980s, when President Gorbachev introduced the policy of *glasnost*.

prominent figure, riding a wave of history over which he had little control? Was he a vicious mass murderer, who cared for nothing but his own glory? Or was he a dictator who forced the Soviet state into the twentieth century for its own good?

Some still hold the determinist view that totalitarianism was inevitable in the USSR. Others insist that the development of the Soviet state could have been different under another leader. There had been several powerful figures opposed to Stalin in the late 1920s and early 1930s. Many of his colleagues, such as Bukharin and Kirov, believed that his policies should have been carried out without

using force. Trotsky disagreed with the policy of "socialism in one country," and argued that the struggle for revolutions in other countries should have continued. If one of these individuals had become the Soviet leader, he would certainly have pursued different policies.

One thing is certain: Stalinism had an immense effect, not only on the Soviet Union but on all the states that fell under its rule, and the millions of people all over the world who have called themselves communists. It is only now, in the late twentieth century, that the system Stalin set up is finally being torn down.

Leading figures

Nikita Khrushchev on a "goodwill visit" to Czechoslovakia in 1957, following the crushing of the Czech uprising by the Soviet Army.

Bukharin, Nicholas I. (1888–1938) Communist leader

One of the more important Marxist theoreticians of his day, Nicholas Bukharin joined the Moscow Committee of Bolsheviks in 1908. He was later arrested and deported. On his return after the Bolshevik revolution, he edited *Pravda* (1917–29) and served on both the Comintern Executive Committee and the Politburo (1924–9). Highly regarded by Lenin and a supporter of the NEP, he backed Stalin against Trotsky in 1924–5, but fell out with the new leader in 1929 over the policy of "eliminating the *kulaks*." Bukharin continued to oppose Stalin on the Party Central Committee until his arrest, trial and execution in 1938.

Kamenev, Lev B. (1883–1936) Bolshevik politician

Although an ardent Bolshevik, Kamenev disapproved of the way the Bolshevik revolution was conducted. After Lenin's death he at first sided with Stalin against Trotsky, then joined with Trotsky and Zinoviev in an unsuccessful bid to prevent Stalin's rise to power. After 1928 he remained peripheral to the Party. Kamenev was arrested and tried in 1935, re-tried the following year, and executed.

Khrushchev, Nikita S. (1894–1971) Soviet leader

Khrushchev was one of the most successful of a generation of loyal Party servants who rose to power and influence during the Stalinist era. The son of a miner from the Ukraine, Khrushchev fought in the Civil War, then worked his way up the Party ladder to become Moscow Party Secretary in 1935. He assisted Stalin in his purges and joined the Politburo in 1939. During World War II he gave political support to military commanders in the Ukraine. He was elected First Secretary of the Party after Stalin's death in 1953. He was later responsible for initiating the policies of destalinization and peaceful coexistence with the West.

Vladimir Lenin in 1920.

Kirov, Sergei M. (1886–1934) Bolshevik politician

Kirov probably came closer to toppling Stalin from power than any other Soviet leader after 1928. He joined the Bolsheviks in 1905, played an important part in extending Soviet power into the Caucasus region after the Bolshevik revolution, and became Leningrad Party Secretary in 1926. A staunch supporter of Stalin, he was admitted to the Politburo in 1930. Four years later, however, he had changed his views and led a movement that opposed the "cult of the individual" that had grown up around Stalin. Kirov's assassination in December 1934, later revealed to have been instigated by Stalin, marked the beginning of the purges of the Party and government, which lasted until the end of the decade.

Lenin, Vladimir I. (1870–1924) Bolshevik leader

Lenin (born Vladimir Ulyanov) studied Marxism and revolutionary tactics from his student days. Exiled in 1897, in 1903 he founded the Bolshevik faction of the Social Democratic Party, in London. He returned briefly to Russia during the 1905 revolution, and again in 1917 to organize the Bolshevik revolution. Lenin was the leader of the new Soviet state until his death in 1924, although for the last year of his life he was considerably weakened by a series of strokes. Shortly before his death he warned the Party not to trust Stalin.

Molotov, Vyacheslav M. (1890–1986) Soviet statesman

Vyacheslav Skriabin, who changed his name to Molotov (the hammer) in 1905, was one of the very few original Bolsheviks who survived the Stalinist era and he continued to serve the USSR into the 1960s. He supported Stalin from 1921 on and was the second most powerful figure in the USSR throughout Stalin's dictatorship. He held a number of key posts, launching the First Five-Year Plan, serving on the Politburo, and acting as Prime Minister from 1930 to 1941. As Commissar for Foreign Affairs (later Foreign Minister) from 1939 to 1956, Molotov was at his most influential. In this post he negotiated the Nazi–Soviet Non-Aggression Pact of August 1939, served as liaison with the Allies after 1941, and built up the Soviet bloc after 1945. Shortly after Khrushchev's seizure of power Molotov was relegated to the post of Ambassador to Mongolia (1957–60). He was dismissed in 1961.

Shostakovich, Dimitri D. (1906–1975) Composer

A gifted and popular composer of music, Dimitri Shostakovich suffered from Party censorship. After being criticized in 1934, when his *Lady Macbeth of Mtsensk* was felt to be "too divorced from the proletariat," he responded with a fifth symphony entitled *A Soviet Artist's Reply to Just Criticism*. The authorities approved of his stirring and patriotic *Leningrad Symphony* of 1942, written to celebrate the city's heroic resistance to the armies of Nazi Germany. Shostakovich fell from favor again when the war was over but became accepted once more after Stalin's death.

Solzhenitsyn, Alexander I. (1918–) Writer

Solzhenitsyn studied mathematics, science and literature before being conscripted into the Army to fight the Nazi invasion of 1941. He served with distinction and was decorated for gallantry. But in 1945 he was arrested by SMERSH, a particularly ruthless branch of the secret police, and accused of criticizing Stalin. His eight years in various labor camps inspired the novel *One Day in the Life of Ivan Denisovich* (1962), a simple but brilliant condemnation of the *Gulag*. The Khrushchev regime approved of attacks on the Stalinist regime, but Solzhenitsyn went on to make more profound observations on the corruption of the whole Soviet system (he published *The First Circle* and *Cancer Ward* in 1968 and *The Gulag Archipelago* in 1973). He was driven into exile in the West in 1974.

Stalin, Joseph V. (1879–1953) Soviet leader

From an impoverished Georgian peasant background, as a young man Joseph Dzhugashvili (later Stalin – "man of steel") joined the Social Democratic Party, where his ability, efficiency and dedication to the cause attracted the attention of Lenin. Although Stalin was clearly an important figure by 1924, at the time few thought that he would take over Lenin's role as Soviet leader. However, employing a mixture of guile and ruthlessness he used his position as Party Secretary to win control over the USSR by 1928. He then proceeded to modernize the state with a series of Five-Year Plans and to destroy all opponents, both real and imaginary. Though badly shaken by the Nazi invasion of 1941, he managed to rally the nation and guide it to victory in 1945. The final years of his life were marked by increasing paranoia and a serious rift with the West, known as the Cold War. Stalin's achievements were considerable, but his methods were so barbaric that he is now almost universally condemned.

Georgi Zhukov.

Trotsky, Leon D. (1879–1940) Bolshevik revolutionary

Until the death of Lenin in 1924, Trotsky (born Lev Bronstein) was the second most important figure in the Russian communist movement. He joined the Menshevik wing of the Social Democratic Party in 1903, and became chairman of the first soviet in St. Petersburg during the 1905 revolution. Trotsky became a Bolshevik in 1917 and played a key role in organizing the second revolution in November. He negotiated the Treaty of Brest-Litovsk (1918) and formed the Red Army during the Civil War. After 1924 leading the Comintern was his principal role, and he became isolated from the internal affairs of the Party; Stalin was therefore easily able to outmaneuver him, and he was forced into exile in 1929. He was murdered by a Stalinist agent in Mexico eleven years later.

Zhukov, Georgi K. (1896–1974) Soviet military leader

Zhukov was the outstanding Soviet military leader of World War II. Of peasant stock, he fought in World War I and the Civil War, and he was then trained in tank warfare by the Germans in the early 1920s. Zhukov earned his reputation fighting Japanese infiltrators in 1939. In the World War that followed he played a major part in the defense of Leningrad, Moscow and Stalingrad, before going on to mastermind the Soviet counter-attack. As Supreme Commander-in-Chief of the Soviet forces, he received the surrender of Berlin in May 1945. Stalin, fearing that Zhukov had become too successful, reduced his responsibilities after World War II, but Zhukov returned to favor in 1953 and became Minister of Defense in 1955.

Important dates

Note:
Until 1918 Russia used the Julian calendar, which was thirteen days behind the rest of Europe. All the dates here are in the Gregorian calendar in use elsewhere in Europe.

Date	Events
1879	Birth of Joseph Dzhugashvili (Stalin).
1899	Stalin expelled from Theological Seminary at Tiflis.
1903	Stalin exiled to Siberia.
1914	Outbreak of World War I.
1917	*March* Czarist government collapses.
	November Bolshevik revolution.
	Stalin becomes First Commissar for the Nationalities.
1918	Treaty of Brest-Litovsk signed and Russia withdraws from war.
	Trotsky appointed Commissar for War.
	Civil War in Russia (to 1922).
1922	Stalin appointed Communist Party Secretary.
	Lenin suffers first stroke.
	Zinoviev, Kamenev and Stalin unite to oppose Trotsky.
	Russia becomes the USSR.
1924	Death of Lenin.
1925	Trotsky removed from Commissariat of War.
	Stalin allies with Bukharin and Rykov against Zinoviev and Kamenev.
1926	Trotsky expelled from Politburo.
1929	Introduction of First Five-Year Plan (to December 1932).
	Stalin supreme political figure in USSR.
	Trotsky exiled from USSR.
	Collectivization and elimination of *kulaks* begins.
	Bukharin expelled from Politburo.
1930	Pace of collectivization of agriculture eased.
1931	Trial of Mensheviks.
1932	Internal passports introduced.
	Widespread famine (to 1934).
1933	Introduction of Second Five-Year Plan (to 1937).
1934	Secret Police (originally CHEKA, now GPU) reorganized as NKVD.
	Assassination of Kirov, Leningrad Party Secretary.
1935	Purges begin.
	"Stakhanovite" labor begins.
	Reintroduction of ranks in Red Army.
1936	Divorce made more difficult.
	Spanish Civil War (to 1939).
	First Show Trial: Zinoviev, Kamenev and other Bolshevik veterans condemned.
	New constitution introduced.

Date	Events
1937	Second Show Trial: seventeen "Trotskyite bandits" condemned. Army leadership purged.
1938	Third Show Trial: Bukharin, Rykov and nineteen others condemned. Introduction of Third Five-Year Plan (to 1941).
1939	Nazi–Soviet Non-Aggression Pact. Outbreak of World War II. Red Army invades eastern Poland. War with Finland (to 1940).
1940	Baltic States annexed.
1941	Germany attacks the USSR in Operation Barbarossa. Stalin appointed Supreme Commander of the Army. Siege of Leningrad (to 1944). Kiev falls to Nazis. Siege of Moscow.
1942	Siege of Stalingrad (to 1943).
1943	Battle of Kursk – Nazis defeated by the Soviet Army. Stalin meets Churchill and Roosevelt at Tehran Conference.
1944	Red Army sweeps through eastern Europe.
1945	Allied leaders meet at Yalta Conference. Red Army enters Berlin; Germany surrenders. Allied leaders meet at Potsdam Conference.
1946	Introduction of Fourth Five-Year Plan (to 1950). Famine in Ukraine (to 1947). Cold War begins.
1947	Truman Doctrine announced. Cominform founded.
1948	Communist coup in Czechoslovakia.
1949	Communists seize power in China. German Democratic Republic formed. USSR explodes atomic bomb. NATO formed by Western nations.
1950	Sino-Soviet Treaty. Korean War (to 1953).
1951	Introduction of Fifth Five-Year Plan (to 1955).
1953	Death of Stalin.
1955	Khrushchev established as new Soviet leader and destalinization begins.
1961	Stalin reburied. *One Day in the Life of Ivan Denisovich* published.

Glossary

Absolutism	A political system in which a dictator or monarch holds unrestricted power.
Blitzkrieg	(Literally "lightning war") An intensive military attack designed to defeat the enemy quickly.
Bolsheviks	(Literally "the majority") The faction of the Social Democratic Party led by Lenin that organized the November 1917 revolution.
Bourgeoisie	The ruling class, in Marxist terms.
Bureaucracy	A government administered by many different bureaus in which action is made difficult by the need to follow complex, rigid rules.
Capitalism	An economic system based on market forces and the right of individuals to own wealth and property.
Cold War	The period of political and military tension between the United States and the Soviet bloc after World War II.
Comintern	The Communist International, set up by the Bolsheviks in 1919 to promote world communism.
Commissar	A communist government officer, before 1946 when the title "minister" was reintroduced.
Communism	A political theory that aims toward a classless society where private ownership has been abolished, in which each person is provided for according to his or her needs.
Conservative	Supporting the existing customs and values, and opposing change.
Constitution	The system of rules by which a government is conducted.
Counter-revolutionary	Against the changes brought about by a revolution.
Czar	The hereditary emperor of Russia.
Dacha	Russian country house.
Democracy	Rule by the people or their elected representatives.
Destalinization	The dismantling of Stalin's system of government.
Doctrine	Something that is believed or taught.
Expropriation	Seizing property for public use.
Faction	A political group within a larger political party.
Fascism	An extreme right-wing philosophy opposed to democracy; it became popular between the wars, especially in Germany, Italy and Spain.
Glasnost	Openness.
Gulag	The network of prisons and forced labor camps in the USSR.
Ideology	A set of beliefs or teachings.
Imperialism	Policy of extending a state's rule over other countries.
Industrialization	The development of industry on a large scale.
Kolkhoz	A collective farm in which all land, livestock and tools are held in common.
Kremlin	The central government of the Soviet Union; also the ancient citadel that houses the government.
Kulak	A rich peasant farmer.

Marxism	The ideas of the German philosopher Karl Marx (1818–83). He claimed to have discovered the laws that govern the behavior of human society in history: societies move from feudalism, through capitalism to socialism, directed by economic forces. He held that most nineteenth-century states were in a capitalist phase, and that revolution was needed to herald in the socialist (communist) era. For its believers, Marxism explains the present and offers hope for the future.
Mausoleum	A large, stately tomb.
Menshevik	A party that was formed when the Social Democratic Party split in 1903.
NEP	The New Economic Policy introduced in 1922 that allowed peasants to sell their produce for profit.
NKVD	The Soviet secret police from 1934 to 1943, when it was divided into the NKVD and the NKGB.
Non-Aggression pact	The pact between Germany and the USSR (August 1939) by which they agreed not to attack each other.
Operation Barbarossa	The code-name for the surprise German invasion of the USSR in June 1941.
Paranoid	Gripped by irrational fear.
Peasant	A poor farmer relying on agricultural labor for a living.
Politburo	The most important policy-making committee of the Soviet Communist Party.
Pragmatist	Someone who advocates behavior according to practical considerations rather than theory or dogma.
Pravda	(Literally "Truth") The official Bolshevik newspaper.
Proletariat	The working classes, especially the industrial workers.
Purge	To get rid of something that is unwanted, for example, political opponents.
Real wages	The purchasing power of wages, not their value in money.
Red Square	The large square in the center of Moscow.
Regime	A system of government.
Republic	A state ruled by the people, without a monarch.
Revolution	A complete and permanent change.
Slav	A member of any of the peoples of eastern Europe or Soviet Asia who speak a Slavonic language.
Social Democratic Party	The Russian revolutionary communist party before the 1917 revolution.
Socialism	An economic theory that holds that the state should own all important means of the production and distribution of wealth. Ultimately indistinguishable from communism.
Soviet	An elected council.
Sovkhoz	A state farm in which all land, livestock and implements are owned by the state.
Stalinism	The system of government created in the USSR by Stalin.
Surplus	A quantity in excess of what is needed.
Totalitarianism	A one-party state with absolute control over every aspect of life.
USSR	The Union of Soviet Socialist Republics.
Utopia	The perfect society.
Whites	The anti-communist groups in Russia after the 1917 Revolution.

Further reading

Easier Books
Alliluyeva, Svetlana, *Twenty Letters to a Friend*, Harper and Row, 1967.
Andreyev, Olga Chernov, *Cold Spring in Russia*, Ardis, 1978.
Blassingame, Wyatt, *Joseph Stalin and Communist Russia*, Garrard, 1971.
Caulkins, Janet, *Joseph Stalin*, Franklin Watts, 1990.
Khrushchev, Nikita, *Khrushchev Remembers*, Little, Brown, 1970.
Marrin, Albert, *Stalin: Russia's Man of Steel*, Penguin, 1988.
Pimlott, T., *Stalin's Russia, 1924–1939*, Macmillan, 1987.

Scholarly Works
Bialer, Seweryn, *Stalin and His Generals: Soviet Military Memoirs of World War II*, Westview, 1984.
Deutscher, I. The *Prophet Outcast: Leon Trotsky 1929–1940*, Oxford University Press, 1963; *Stalin*, Oxford University Press, 1967.
Medvedev, R.A., *Let History Judge*, Random House, 1973; *On Stalin and Stalinism*, Oxford University Press, 1979.
Rigby, T.H., *Stalin*, Prentice-Hall, 1966.
Souvarine, Boris, *Stalinism: A Critical Survey of Bolshevism*, Octagon Books, 1972.
Tucker, R.C., (ed.), *Stalinism: Essays in Historical Interpretation*, Norton, 1978.
Ulam, A.B., *Stalin: The Man and His Era*, Beacon, 1987.
Zaleski, E. *Stalinist Planning for Economic Growth, 1933–1952*, Macmillan, 1980.

Original Sources
Alliluyeva, Svetlana, *Only One Year*, Harper & Row, 1969.
Djilas, Milovan, *Conversations with Stalin*, Harcourt, Brace, World, 1962.
Reed, John, *Ten Days That Shook the World*, Modern Library, 1935.
Solzhenitsyn, A., *Cancer Ward*, Modern Library, 1983; *The Gulag Archipelago,* Harper and Row, 1985; *One Day in the Life of Ivan Denisovich*, Signet Classics, 1963.
Stalin, J., *Problems of Leninism*, Moscow, 1945.
Trotsky, L., *Stalin: An Appraisal of the Man and His Influences*, Scarborough House, 1970.

Notes on sources

1 Cited in Shub, D., *Lenin: A Biography,* Penguin, 1966, pp.434–5.
2 Cited in Payne, R., *The Rise and Fall of Stalin,* W.H. Allen, 1966, p.101.
3 *Ibid.,* p.343.
4 Stalin, J., *Problems of Leninism,* Moscow, 1953, pp.97 & 106.
5 Deutscher, I., *Stalin,* Penguin, 1966, p.318.
6 McCauley, *Stalin and Stalinism,* Longman, 1983, p.20.
7 *Ibid.,* p.15.
8 Statistics based on Cook, C. and Stevenson, J., *Handbook of Modern European History,* Longman, 1987, Section IV.
9 Stalin *op. cit.,* p.456.
10 Riasanovsky, N., *A History of Russia,* Oxford, 1977, pp.547–557 and McCauley *op. cit.,* pp.23–31.
11 Riasanovsky *op. cit.,* p.547.
12 Hosking, G., *History of the Soviet Union,* Collins, 1985, p.482.
13 Cook and Stevenson *op. cit.,* Section IV.
14 Hosking *op. cit.,* p.482.
15 *Ibid.,* p.482.
16 McCauley *op. cit.,* p.30.
17 Cited in Harrison, S.M., *World Conflict in the Twentieth Century,* Macmillan, 1987, p.142.
18 Riasanovsky *op. cit.,* p.549.
19 Stalin *op. cit.,* p.405.
20 Riasanovsky *op. cit.,* p.552.
21 *Ibid.* p.552.
22 *Ibid.,* p.555, and McCauley *op. cit.,* p.29.
23 Zaleski, E., *Stalinist Planning for Economic Growth 1933–1952,* Macmillan, 1980, p.503.
24 Hosking *op. cit.,* p.482.
25 Riasanovsky *op. cit.,* p.551.
26 Nichol, J. and Shephard, K., *Russia,* Blackwell, 1986, p.36.
27 Stalin *op. cit.,* p.415.
28 *Ibid.,* p.418.
29 Marx, K. and Engels, F., *The Communist Manifesto,* Penguin, 1985, p.105.
30 Stalin *op. cit.,* p.631.
31 McCauley *op. cit.,* p.33.
32 Hosking *op. cit.,* p.195.
33 Cited in Payne *op. cit.,* p.428.
34 Stalin *op. cit.,* p.778.
35 Hosking *op. cit.,* p.203.
36 Riasanovsky *op. cit.,* p.634.
37 Cook and Stevenson *op. cit.,* Section IV.
38 Cited in Hosking *op. cit.,* p.213.
39 *Ibid.,* p.205.
40 Stalin *op. cit.,* p.700.
41 Hosking *op. cit.,* p.235.
42 *Ibid.,* p.239.
43 Mandelstam, N., *Hope Against Hope,* Collins, 1971, p.13.
44 Stalin *op. cit.,* p.700.
45 Hosking *op cit.,* p.219.
46 Stalin *op. cit.,* pp.584 & 594.
47 Medvedev, R., *Let History Judge,* Knopf, 1971, pp.441–2.
48 McCauley *op. cit.,* p.49.
49 Cited in Nichol and Shephard *op. cit.,* p.49.
50 Riasanovsky *op. cit.,* p.585; McCauley *op. cit.,* p.65.
51 Hosking *op. cit.,* pp.482–3.
52 Zaleski *op. cit.,* p.503.
53 McCauley *op. cit.,* pp.100–101.
54 Cited in Deutscher, *op. cit.,* p.599.
55 Cited in *ibid.,* pp.595–6.
56 Cited in *ibid.,* pp.595–6.
57 Cited in Payne *op. cit.,* p.620.
58 Hofstadter, R. (ed.), *Great Issues in American History from Reconstruction to the Present Day,* Vintage, 1969, p.414.
59 Cited in Payne, *op. cit.,* p.682.
60 Official decree, in *ibid.,* p.713.
61 Medvedev *op. cit.,* p.563.
62 Hosking *op. cit.,* pp. 482–3.
63 Cited in Tucker, R.C., *Stalinism,* Norton, 1977, p.235.
64 Tucker *op. cit.,* pp.719–20.
65 Tucker *op. cit.,* p.612.
66 Tucker *op. cit.,* p.77.

Index

Acknowledgments

The author and publishers would like to thank the following for allowing their illustrations to be reproduced in this book: Associated Press 47; British Library 31; Mary Evans Picture Library *cover*, 25 (top), 28, 29, 44; E T Archive 10, 11; John Freeman & Co. 13 (top), 16, 17, 21; John Frost 51; Peter Newark 4 (both), 6, 8, 13 (bottom), 23, 26, 33, 35, 37, 40, 53, 55; Mansell Collection 36; Novosti Press Agency 12, 15; Popperfoto 18, 38, 39, 43, 52; Topham Picture Library 7, 9, 14, 20, 22, 24, 25 (bottom), 30, 32, 34, 41, 42, 46, 49, 50; Wayland Picture Library 19, 27, 48. The maps were supplied by Peter Bull Art Studio. Artwork on page 20 by Jenny Hughes.

The index was compiled by Indexing Specialists, Hove, East Sussex.

The publishers would like to thank Collins for permitting us to quote from *Hope Against Hope* by N. Mandelstam, 1971.